The Biography of Me

A Journey of Self-Discovery

by Diane P. Kostick

illustrated by Shelly Rasche

Cover by Jeff Van Kanegan

Copyright © 1992, Good Apple

ISBN No. 0-86653-687-6

Printing No. 987654

Good Apple
1204 Buchanan, Box 299
Carthage, IL 62321-0299

S I M O N & S C H U S T E R *A Paramount Communications Company*

Dedication

This book is dedicated with all my affection and gratitude to Andy, Yuri and Jolie.

Special thanks to the following people for their editing skills, moral support, technical assistance and sage advice:

April Montgomery
Rob Luby
Bob Baker
Bob Soule
Middle School Custodial Staff who "opened" many a door for me
Barrington Writers Workshop members
My English students who piloted the book and assisted me in ferreting the "beasts" out of it

I dedicate my book to_____.

My name is _____.

Today's date is _____.

Table of Contents

Introduction 1

User's Guide...3

Take a Look at Me 6

Birth Announcement 7

Who Am I?..8

I Am Unique..13

My Name Is Special...24

Monday's Child 29

My Family 30

My House 32

My Room 33

Where I Live 34

My History in Pictures 38

My Family Tree...41

My Uncles, Aunts, and Cousins

   Paternal Side of Family 46

   Maternal Side of Family 48

Where in the World? 50

Where in the World? A Mini Research Report 51

My State on the Map 54

My Time Line..57

Family Customs..58

Favorite Family Recipe 63

Myths, Legends, and Folktales..65

Tell Me a Story… 70

Did You Ever? 72

Across Generations 75

Cost of Living..80

Comparative Cost of Living 83

Family Heirlooms 85

Heraldry..91

My Coat of Arms...97

My Coat of Arms–My Shield 99

My Medieval Manor 100

My Hobbies and Collections...101

Memories 105

School Days..107

My Favorite Things 112

Friends and Friendship...114
My Circle of Life...119
Pets..121
My Heroes..124
Remembering Someone Special 132
An Acrostic...134
My Acrostic 135
Me Collage 136
I Have Changed 137
Someday I Want to Be 140
Autographs..143
Poem for Reflection...145
My Keepsake Page...146
Glossary 147
Bibliography..152

iv

GA1421

Introduction

Know thyself.
Plutarch

Writing your autobiography is fun and fascinating. It enables you to look at the past, while it demands you look to the future. Doing a thorough job on this personal quest requires that you be as shrewd as Sherlock Holmes, as scientific as Madame Curie and as colorful as Salvador Dali; but the rewards are incalculable.

When you take the time to examine "who you are," to gather data about your forebearers and to reflect on your future, you will surely get "hooked" on recording your memories, sharing your thoughts and expressing your feelings. In addition, you will join legions of other "voyagers" called genealogists who are searching for their own family data in dark church basements; in drafty, old courthouse buildings; or in libraries especially equipped to help them investigate their families' heroes, history and heritage.

How old should you be when you start writing your autobiography? That is a difficult question to answer. Some people feel you should begin when you retire; others feel that it is okay to start as soon as you are old enough to pick up a pencil and begin scribbling your "life's story" on a piece of paper or the wall near your crib.

The only thing that is certain is that we need to record our thoughts, feelings and experiences as soon as they happen, because our minds play tricks on us, and what we thought we'd remember for the rest of our lives, we begin to forget as each day's sun sinks beneath the horizon.

Filling in the pages of this book while the events are "fresh" in your memory will enable you to leave a vivid account of your life for this generation, and it will enable you to tell future generations about you, about important events in your life and the role you have played in history.

GA1421

To help you complete parts of your autobiography, it will be necessary to seek assistance from other family members. You will be required to ask your parents, (stepparents or guardians), grandparents, relatives and friends to help you research and remember the events that have made you cry, the moments that have made you laugh, and the people, places and things which are essential to your personal history.

Have fun working through the pages of this book, and keep in mind that you are completing this book first for yourself, then for your immediate family and finally for generations to come.

GA1421

User's Guide

This autobiography is designed to enable you to reflect on the past, think about the present and plan for the future. It will assist you in gathering information about your famous and not-so-famous forebearers and launch you on a lifelong odyssey of self-discovery. Because of the importance of this book, take time to muse over your thoughts before you commit them to paper, and keep in mind that what you write will become your history for generations to come. So that anyone who reads your book will understand the abbreviations, symbols and dating techniques you have used in your book, adhere to the following list of guidelines.

1. Enter all dates in this fashion:

Day	Month	Year
4	July	1776

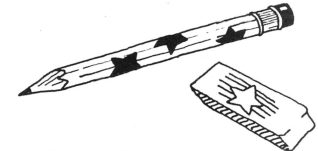

2. Add "lines" for additional family members, reflective pieces or whenever needed. For example, on the "Who Am I?" pages, you might need to list stepparents, their occupations and their off-spring. If you need to add lines for this additional data or if you need to add space to any part of your autobiography, feel free to do so.

3. When entering a married woman's name, indicate her maiden name by placing it in parentheses as follows:
   Mary (Jones) Smith

4. Use the following key for data entered:
   ca.– "about," also seen as "circa" and is used when dates are not precisely known

   cont.–continuation, used for family tree data which may be spread beyond the number of pages provided or anywhere in the book in which you must go on to another page

   b.–date of birth

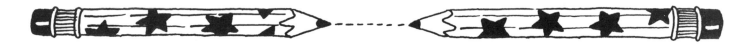

p.b.–place of birth

m.–date of marriage

p.m.–place of marriage

d.–date of death

p.d.–place of death

s.–spouse

re.–remarriage

5. Record places such as city (county) state in the following manner:

Chicago (Cook) Illinois

6. On the birth certificate page, if you were not born in the United States, when it asks about the "country" in which you were born, substitute the appropriate political division name used in the country in which you were born. For example, the area might be referred to as a province, district, parish, region, canton or the like. If you are not sure what the division is called, check a geographical dictionary for the correct term to use. This information is important if you want to send for any records from another country. Then if you were not born in the United States, be sure to enter the name of the country in which you were born in the appropriate space on your "birth certificate."

7. The term *illustrate* used anywhere in the book, means you may draw, paste cutout pictures in place in the book, add photos or generate computer graphics. Precious family photos may be photocopied, colored and placed as needed in your book in lieu of using photos which you prefer to keep in another place.

8. The term *write* means to do by hand, typewriter or computer. Typewritten or computer-prepared pieces can be printed, and then cut and pasted in your book.

GA1421

9. Any family remarriages should be indicated with a "rm." notation, and other pertinent information about your "new" family should be included in your autobiography.

10. When listing names on your "family tree," your paternal or maternal charts, or anywhere throughout your autobiography, always put the needed names in chronological birth order. That means list the oldest person first and the youngest person last.

11. Color all the graphics on each page in your book. This makes your book as unique as you are. You may wish to use markers, colored pencils or watercolors. Just be careful that whatever you use does not "bleed" on to the next page. If you place a piece of paper between the page you are working on and the next page, this will prevent "accidents."

GA1421

Take a Look at Me

On this page, draw a self-portrait or put a recent photo of yourself.

Acclaim the birth of

_____
(your legal name)

a child of _____
*(biological father)

and _____
*(biological mother)

born on _____
(month and day)

in the year _____

in the city of_____

in the county of _____

in the state of _____

in the country of _____

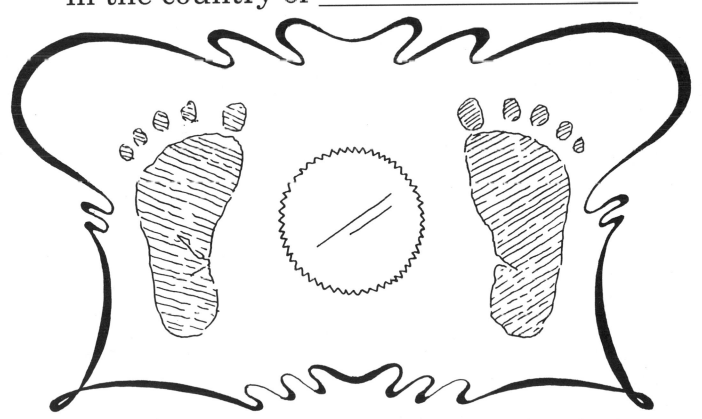

*If data about biological parents is unknown, in pencil write
Unknown at this time on the lines.

7

GA1421

Who Am I?

No person would, I think exchange their existence with any other person, however fortunate.

Hazlitt

1. My name is _____ .

2. My street address is _____ .

   My town is _____ state _____ zip _____ .

3. Age _____ My birthday is _____ .
   (day, month, year)

4. Color of my eyes _____ Color of my hair _____

5. My height _____ My weight _____

6. My *father's name is _____ .

7. My *father's occupation is _____ .

8. My *mother's name is _____ .

9. My *mother's occupation is _____ .

10. I am the _____ child in my family.
    (first, last, middle,**only)

    I like (do not like) being the _____ child in my family

    because _____ .

*Add information for stepparents as appropriate.
**Omit #'s 11 and 12

8

GA1421

11. The names and ages of my **brothers are

               Name   Birth Date

a. _____   _____

b. _____   _____

c. _____   _____

12. The names and ages of my **sisters are

               Name   Birth Date

a. _____   _____

b. _____   _____

c. _____   _____

13. My paternal ***grandfather's name is_____.

He lives in _____.

14. My paternal ***grandmother's name is _____.

She lives in _____.

15. My ***maternal grandfather's name is _____.

He lives in _____.

16. My ***maternal grandmother's name is _____.

She lives in _____.

**Add the names of step-siblings as appropriate.

***If a grandparent or parent is deceased, indicate that by writing "d" and the date of his/her death after his/her name. If grandparents have remarried, you may wish to write the name of their current spouses on the appropriate lines, and write "re." after their names. Include the dates of the new marriages, too.

          GA1421

17. Write a theme entitled "Who Am I?" You might like to begin this activity by making a list of words or phrases that you think describe your appearance, things you like to do in your leisure time, foods you like to eat, places you like to vacation, and other essential information you would like your audience to know about you. The theme can be funny or sad, factual or fanciful; it can be the way you see yourself or the way you think others see you.

Who Am I?

?

?

?

?

_____

_____

_____

_____

_____

_____

_____

_____

_____

_____

_____

_____

? ?

_____
_____
_____
_____
? ?

_____
_____
_____
? ?

_____
_____
_____
? ?

_____
_____
_____
? ?

_____
_____
_____
? ?

_____
_____
_____

GA1421

18. This is a picture of me (or put a picture of someone you think you might like to look like if you could).

19. I started this autobiography on _____.
(day, month, year)

12

# I Am Unique

*Life teaches us to be less harsh with our-
selves and with others.*

Goethe

The Census Bureau tells us that there are over five billion people
in the world. Among them, you are one of a kind. Like all living
things–snowflakes, roses, zebras and even fingerprints–you are
unique. From your parents you have been given a set of biological
and psychological characteristics which have gone together to
make you who you are. In addition, you have developed your own
unique personality traits which are quite independent of your
parental gene pool.

Your parental, or biological, heritage is easy to see. All you need to
do is glance at members of your family gathered around the
dinner table, and you can readily see the common features you
share with them. Further evidence of how you participate in your
family "gene pool" is seen as you flip through pages of any family
photo albums and detect specific features you share with others in
your extended family. For example, you might have acquired their
high cheek bones, their round faces, their angular noses, their
above average height or their many rust-colored freckles. Another
way in which you can take stock of your physical inheritance is to
stand in front of a mirror and get a good look at yourself. Take a
moment and carefully inspect the color of your eyes, the texture of
your hair, the length of your bones, the height of your forehead,
the shape of your chin and any other readily recognizable physical
features which you share with other members of your family.
After all, your biology is a part of who you are. It is the quickest
way to see how you relate to others in your immediate and
extended biological family–your parents, siblings, grandparents,
aunts, uncles and the like.

Your physical similarities are quite easy to spot. But you are more
than the sum of these inherited features. You are also someone
with your own one-of-a-kind feelings, needs and hopes for the
future. These harder-to-observe traits make up your personality
which has been honed from years of living with your family,
associating with your friends and responding in your own way to
the world around you. Finding out what kind of personality you
have is harder to "see," and may take you more time to determine
how you are like members of your family and how you are not like
them at all. The following lists may help you see your physical
family likenesses, and they may help you recognize ways in which
you are unique.

GA1421

Below you will find two lists of terms which will help you examine your biological and psychological characteristics. Column 1 lists physical features and mannerisms, and Column 2 lists personality traits and other general characteristics. Look over both lists. Then with a marker or pen, highlight or put a check next to those items which you think describe you. These check marks enable you to fill in the pages which follow, and they will serve as a handy guide as you explore more ways to knowing just who you are.

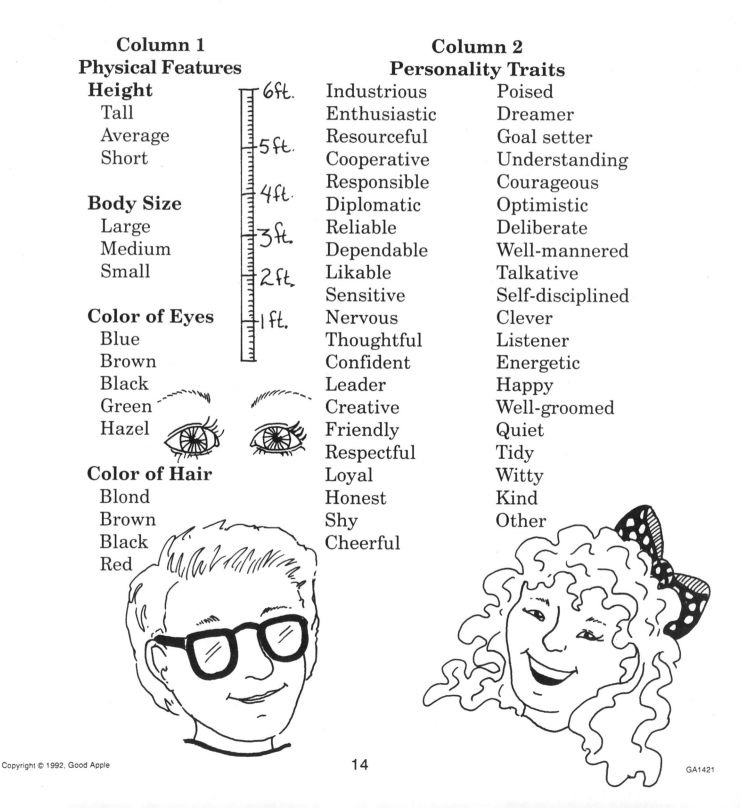

Column 1
Physical Features

Height
- Tall
- Average
- Short

6ft.
5ft.
4ft.
3ft.
2ft.
1ft.

Body Size
- Large
- Medium
- Small

Color of Eyes
- Blue
- Brown
- Black
- Green
- Hazel

Color of Hair
- Blond
- Brown
- Black
- Red

Column 2
Personality Traits

Industrious	Poised
Enthusiastic	Dreamer
Resourceful	Goal setter
Cooperative	Understanding
Responsible	Courageous
Diplomatic	Optimistic
Reliable	Deliberate
Dependable	Well-mannered
Likable	Talkative
Sensitive	Self-disciplined
Nervous	Clever
Thoughtful	Listener
Confident	Energetic
Leader	Happy
Creative	Well-groomed
Friendly	Quiet
Respectful	Tidy
Loyal	Witty
Honest	Kind
Shy	Other
Cheerful	

GA1421

Shape of Head
Oval
Round
Triangular

Other Characteristics
Athletic	Scientific
Artistic	Verbal
Day person	Night person

Mannerisms
Crack knuckles
Chew fingernails
Tap pen/pencil
Play with hair or twist it around your fingers
Pretend to drive a car with appropriate sounds
Fiddle with buttons on blouse or shirt
Hum

1. The physical features I have inherited are

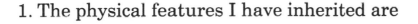

Traits	**Inherited from** (name of person)
a. _____	_____
b. _____	_____
c. _____	_____

2. On the next page, write a poem entitled "A Portrait of …" (write your name after *of* as fancy as you wish). What you should imagine is that you are introducing yourself to someone who doesn't know you. It would be a good idea to use a number of the characters from the lists above to help you compose your self-portrait. Then, when you have finished your poem, you should appear to "walk off" the page to greet the "stranger" waiting to meet you. The style of the poem is up to you. It may rhyme, it may be a narrative (story) or it may be free verse. Note that you will be writing an acrostic form of poem later, so save that kind until then.

GA1421

A Portrait of _____

_____

_____

_____

_____

_____

_____

_____

_____

_____

_____

_____

_____

_____

3. Three things I am especially good at are

   a. _____

   b. _____

   c. _____

4. Three things I like about myself are

   a. _____

   b. _____

   c. _____

5. Three things other people say I do well are

   a. _____

   b. _____

   c. _____

GA1421

6. I am proud of

a. _____ because

_____

b. _____ because

_____

c. _____ because

_____

7. The best thing about me is _____

_____

_____

_____

*This is a picture of me when I was born.

*If a photo is not available, use magazine cutouts or draw your own pictures to represent what you looked like when you were born and what you look like now.

18

8. *I know this about my birth (time, place, etc.).

_____

_____

_____

_____

_____

_____

_____

_____

_____

_____

_____

_____

_____

*If this information is unknown at this time, in pencil write *Unknown* on the top line.

GA1421

9. Describe your favorite toy or "friend" you had as a child. Was it a special blanket, book or stuffed animal? What name did you give it? Did a relative or friend give it to you? Was it given to you for a special occasion? Try to recall as many vivid details about your "special friend" as you can. Use the wonderful tale of childhood called *The Velveteen Rabbit* as a model for your description. If you haven't read the book, get a copy. You will enjoy this classic and no doubt be reminded of what your special toy or friend of childhood meant to you.

_____

_____

_____

_____

_____

_____

_____

_____

_____

_____

_____

_____

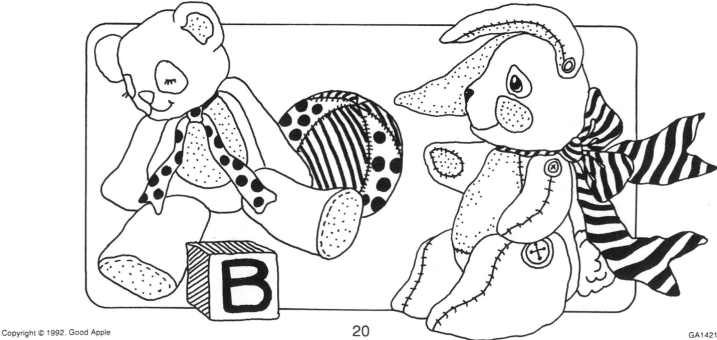

GA1421

10. In the space provided, draw a picture or put an old picture your family might have of your favorite childhood "friend."

11. Lay your hand in the box below. Trace around it. Your hand is another part of you which is unique. Some hands are long and have narrow fingers; some hands are short and have thick fingers; some hands are round and have long fingers and the like. Most people have two different-sized hands because the one they use the most is usually larger than the one they use the least. In fact, our hands, like the rest of us, are unique. After you have traced your hand, list two things that you do well with your hands.

GA1421

12. Two things I do well with my hands are

a. _____

b. _____

13. Circle one: I am right-handed, left-handed, ambidextrous.

14. On line "a." print your name. On line "b." write your name in cursive. Your signature is another way in which you are unlike anyone else.

a. _____
(print your name)

b. _____
(write your name)

15. How old were you when you first started doing chores around the house? _____

16. Name two chores you do.

a. _____

b. _____

17. Get an inked stamp pad and make a copy of your thumbprint. Each of your fingers and thumbs has its own pattern. No one else in the world has the same fingerprint pattern, adding to your uniqueness. After you have copied your special thumb and/or fingerprints, you may enjoy giving your prints "faces" and/or animal shapes which will enable you to express who you are in another way.

GA1421

My Name Is Special

What's in a name?
That which we call a rose
By any other name would smell as sweet.
Shakespeare

Before you were born, your parents gave much thought to the name they would give you. They knew your name would become a vital part of you for the rest of your life. They knew your name would be special, symbolic, and a sign of your uniqueness.

Your surname, or family name, often tells something about your ethnic background or the country from which your ancestors came to America. It may also be a clue to the occupation your family once held. Long ago in Europe, people acquired surnames from the work they did. Someone who grew wheat was called "Farmer"; someone who ground the wheat into flour at a mill was called "Miller"; and someone who baked the flour into bread was called "Baker." Over time, these names stuck with families because it was customary for children to follow in their parents' footsteps and do their parents' work.

On the other hand, the Japanese acquired their surnames from where they lived. Family groups stayed in the same village for generations and took on the name of the area in which they resided. Today, many Japanese families have moved away from the tiny villages and beautiful countryside regions from which their surnames originated, but their names still tell where the families once lived. In Japanese, the word *saka* means "hill" and the word *moto* means "at the foot of," so the name *Sakamoto* means the "family at the foot of the hill."

Given, or first names, came to describe a person's characteristics. The name Leo came from the Latin word for *lion*. So boys were perhaps named Leo because someone in the family by that name was thought to be "strong, dominate, and forceful." On the other hand, the name Patricia comes from the Greek and means "of the nobility," since Greeks of nobility were referred to as "patricians."

24

You might have acquired your given name not because of its meaning but according to a family tradition. For instance, in Greek families, the first boy is always named after the paternal grandfather. Whereas in Russian families, children take their father's name for their middle name. Boys add "vich" to the end of their father's name, while girls add "ova" to it. Thus, the name, "Yuri Andreyevich," means "Yuri, the son of Andrew." This system of naming children enabled Russian parents to keep "tabs" on their children, and it assured that village people would report their children to their parents if the children were seen misbehaving. Most cultures have traditional ways for naming children. Perhaps you were given your name for cultural or traditional reasons. Ask someone in your family to tell you the origin of your given and surnames.

In addition to your given or first name, and your family or surname, you might also have a nickname. Nicknames come about because we have a tendency to shorten names. Sometimes nicknames are given because a younger child in the family is unable to pronounce the name correctly, and sometimes nicknames are bestowed upon people as terms of endearment. Whatever the reason for your nickname, it, too, sets you apart; it makes you special.

1. My full name is _____.

2. My given name is _____, and it means

_____.

3. My surname is _____, and it means

_____.

4. I was given my first name because _____

_____

_____.

25

GA1421

5. Do you think your given name fits you? Yes or no? Why or why not?

_____

_____

_____

6. If I could have selected my first name, the name I would have picked would be _____ because _____

_____

7. My nickname is _____ . If you do not have a nickname, write a nickname you would like to have on the line.

_____

8. How did you get your nickname? If you picked your own nickname, why did you select it?

_____

_____

Immigrants arriving in America in the last part of the nineteenth century were often forced to change their names. Sometimes this came about because officials at the ports of entry were unable to pronounce the person's name correctly, and names were changed because it was believed that doing so would help the new Americans fit better into their adopted society. Knowing the ethnic origin of your name gives you more information about your family and you.

GA1421

9. From what country did your name originate? _____

10. List two famous people with your given name.

    a. _____

    b. _____

11. Name two famous people with your surname.

    a. _____

    b. _____

12. According to the American Name Society, these are the top ten male and female names in America today. If your name appears in the list, highlight it with a marker.

Male Name	Female Names
1. Michael	1. Jennifer
2. Jason	2. Mary
3. Matthew	3. Karen
4. David	4. Michelle
5. Brian	5. Jessica
6. Christopher	6. Katherine
7. John	7. Rebecca
8. James	8. Deborah
9. Jeffery	9. Robin
10. Daniel	10. Megan

GA1421

13. Twenty popular names and what they mean are listed below. If your name and its meaning appear in the list, highlight it with a marker.

Name
1. Adam
2. Andrew
3. Ann
4. Amelia
5. Basil
6. Barbara
7. Brian
8. Camille
9. Cynthia
10. Charles
11. Dan
12. David
13. Dorothy
14. Donald
15. Elizabeth
16. Emily
17. Eileen
18. James
19. Kevin
20. Mary

Meaning
1. Earth
2. Manly
3. Grace
4. Industrious
5. Most noble
6. Stranger
7. Strong
8. Free-born
9. Of the moon
10. To become adult
11. He judged
12. Beloved
13. Gift of God
14. A lord
15. Oath of God
16. Industrious
17. Light
18. May God protect
19. Gentle and beloved
20. Bitter

14. Use the space below to illustrate your name. You may want to write it in hieroglyphics, Morse Code, calligraphy, Greek, or in a secret message manner such as this: +*?@#$. Cut out individual letters for your name from a newspaper or magazine, or, if you prefer, design your own name design in any fashion that you think represents you.

GA1421

Monday's Child

Monday's child is fair of face,
Tuesday's child is full of grace,
Wednesday's child is full of woe,
Thursday's child has far to go,
Friday's child is loving and giving,
Saturday's child works hard for his living,
And the child that is born on the Sabbath day
Is bonny and blithe, and good and gay.

                                        Anonymous

Use a highlighter to draw a line through the phrase in the poem
that indicates the day of the week on which you were born.

My Family

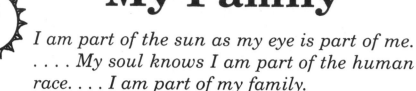

I am part of the sun as my eye is part of me.
. . . . My soul knows I am part of the human
race. . . . I am part of my family.
David H. Lawrence

Make an illustration or put a photo of your family below. Identify each person in the picture. Then on the next sheet "introduce" your family. Give specific personal details about each member and let the reader get to know your family "through your verbal eyes."

GA1421

My Family

31

GA1421

My House

Draw a picture or put a photo below.

GA1421

My Room

Draw a picture or put a photo below.

Where I Live

Virtue is not left to stand alone. He who practices it will have neighbors.

Confucius

1. I live _____.
   (state, city or town)

2. I have lived here for _____.
   (amount of time)

3. Put a photo or draw a picture of your neighborhood in the space below.

34

4. Describe where you live. Is it an urban or rural setting? What are the homes like in your neighborhood?

_____

_____

_____

5. Tell about the best experience you have had living where you do, or write about the oldest memory you have about living there.

_____

_____

_____

_____

_____

_____

_____

_____

_____

_____

GA1421

6. Four interesting historical facts about my city (town) are

a. _____

b. _____

c. _____

d. _____

7. Have you ever moved? If you have not moved, have you ever gone to a new school? Describe what it felt like to move and leave old friends; tell how you felt the first time you entered your new house or school. Recall the new smells, sights, and sounds. If you have never moved, ask someone in your family to recall his/her most difficult move and relate the "moving" story below.

_____

_____

_____

_____

_____

_____

_____

_____

_____

_____

GA1421

8. Tell about the best adventure you have had living where you do. Perhaps it was on a snowy day or during the middle of summer. Who was with you at the time? What were you doing that made it so much fun?

_____

_____

_____

_____

_____

9. If you could live anywhere in the world, where would you pick and why would you select this place?

_____

_____

_____

_____

_____

_____

_____

_____

_____

My History in Pictures

No two days are alike. Take a quick survey of the days and years of your life, and think of the "landmark" events which have affected you in profound ways. They may have made you happy or sad, proud or embarrassed, or they may have made you upset or at peace with yourself. Then from your life's "chronology," select two or three events which vividly "stick out" in your mind. Illustrate each event through photos or drawings, identify the people you were with when the event took place, and explain what happened to you to make it a **memorable** experience.

GA1421

GA1421

My Family Tree

One always retains the trace of one's origins.
Renan

Genealogy, or the study of one's ancestors, is one of the oldest pursuits of mankind. Primitive people worshiped animals as their ancestors. Among the animals they honored were the pig, cow, water buffalo, snake, and eagle. Later Greeks, Romans, and Phoenicians idolized gods and goddesses as their ancestors. The activities of these "superhuman" gods and goddesses were chronicled in stories called myths which have been handed down to us and are widely read today.

Today in America well over five million people are actively engaged in genealogical research. They are looking for information about their ancestors in dust-covered books found in public and private libraries, in dank, dark rooms located in basements of county courthouses, or in boxes in church archives all over the world.

While investigating data about their ancestry, most of these heritage-seekers catch the "genealogy bug" and become "hooked" on gathering as much information as they possibly can. They will go great distances just to find more pieces to their "genealogical puzzle."

The most helpful documents for finding out facts about one's ancestors are birth, baptismal, marriage, and death certificates. But often a great deal of family history is readily available in the front pages of the family Bible or in a family album dutifully documented by some caring family member. Often the mother or grandmother has this task and wisely records the name, weight, and place of birth of all children and grandchildren. Ask your parents to see your family's records and use this information to complete the next parts of your book.

41

GA1421

Another good source of family history is found in diaries, letters, or journals written by a member of this and previous generations. Ask your family to allow you to read these "primary source" materials. They will give you great insight into the everyday activities of your forebearers as well as the outline for the monumental events that happened in their lifetimes.

1. Tell how your oldest known relative came to America. When did this person come? From where did this person come? How did this person get to America? Why did this person journey to the states?

_____

_____

_____

_____

_____

_____

_____

_____

_____

2. When your first known relative came to America, where did he/she live? What kind of job did he/she have?

_____

_____

_____

3. In your opinion, who is the most interesting person in your family? Why?

_____

_____

_____

_____

_____

_____

_____

4. If possible, put a photo of your most interesting relative below. If a photo is not available, draw a picture of what the person looked like, or what you think the person looked like.

43

5. If I could meet my ancestors, this is what I would tell them about my life and the times in which I am living. Call it *"Things I Would Like to Tell My Ancestors."

_____

_____

_____

_____

_____

_____

_____

_____

_____

_____

_____

_____

_____

*You might like to tell your ancestors what it is like to live on the brink of the twenty-first century, or what are the most important news items of the day, or what it is like to be someone growing up today, or about the greatest day of your life, or about whatever you think they would like to know about you and the times in which you live.

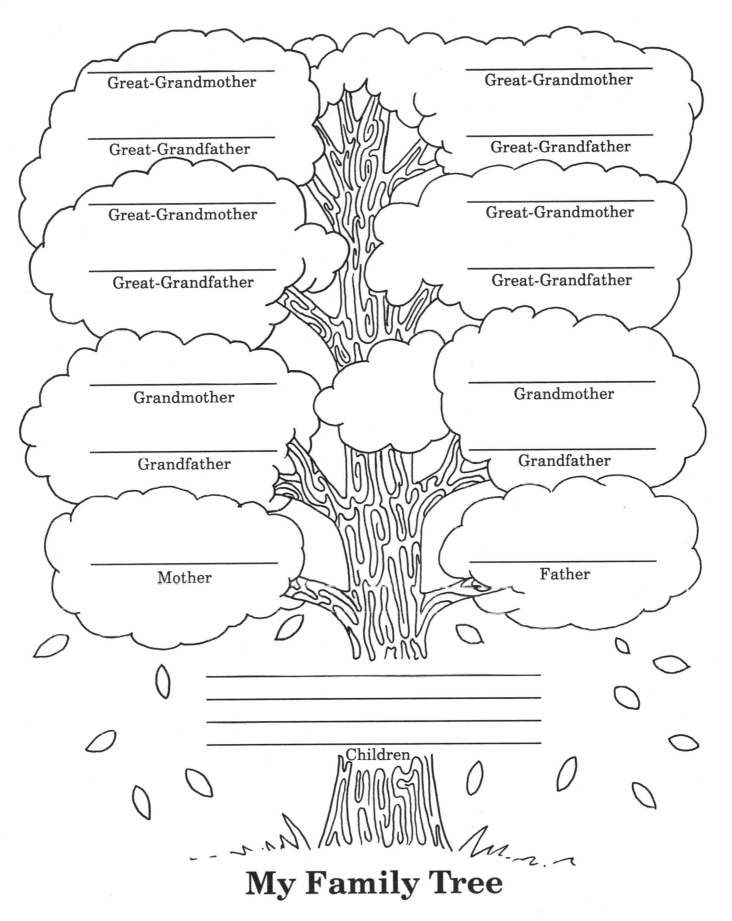

Great-Grandmother

Great-Grandfather

Great-Grandmother

Great-Grandfather

Great-Grandmother

Great-Grandfather

Great-Grandmother

Great-Grandfather

Grandmother

Grandfather

Grandmother

Grandfather

Mother

Father

Children

My Family Tree

Write the name and birth date for each relative. Indicate deceased with (d.) and the date.

45

GA1421

My Uncles, Aunts, and Cousins

(Paternal Side)

Write the name and birthday (day, month, year) of your father's brothers and sisters on the lines by the numbers. On the lines marked "S," write the names and birthdays (day, month, year) of their spouses. On the lines to the right of their names, write the names and birthdays (day, month, year) of their children (your cousins). Write the name of any deceased member of the family on the line, and after the name write "d.," and indicate the date of the person's death. List uncles and aunts with the eldest member of the family first. If your father is an only child, indicate that by writing *only child* on the first line of this "cousin chart."

Uncles and Aunts   **Cousins**

1. _____

    S _____

2. _____

    S _____

3. _____

    S _____

4. _____

    S _____

GA1421

5. _____

   S _____

6. _____

   S _____

7. _____

   S _____

8. _____

   S _____

GA1421

My Uncles, Aunts, and Cousins

(Maternal Side)

Write the name and birthday (day, month, year) of your mother's brothers and sisters on the lines by the numbers. On the lines marked "S," write the names and birthdays (day, month, year) of their spouses. On the lines to the right of their names, write the names and birthdays (day, month, year) of their children (your cousins). Write the name of any deceased member of the family on the line, and after the name write "d.," and indicate the date of the person's death. List uncles and aunts with the eldest member of the family first. If your mother is an only child, indicate that by writing *only child* on the first line of this "cousin chart."

Uncles and Aunts	Cousins
1. _____	
S _____	
2. _____	
S _____	
3. _____	
S _____	
4. _____	
S _____	

GA1421

5. _____

S _____

|_____|
|_____|

6. _____

S _____

|_____|
|_____|

7. _____

S _____

|_____|
|_____|

8. _____

S _____

|_____|
|_____|

Where in the World?

1. Outline areas of the map **blue** to show the country or countries from which your **paternal** ancestors came to America. Write the name or names on the line.

_____

2. Color areas of the map **orange** to show the country or countries from which your **maternal** ancestors came to America. Write the name or names on the line.

_____

3. If **both** paternal and maternal ancestors came from the same country, color the country **blue**, and use a black thin felt marker to make **slash lines** on top of the country you colored blue.

4. On the next several pages, write a mini report on a country from which your ancestors came. The country I will research is

_____ .

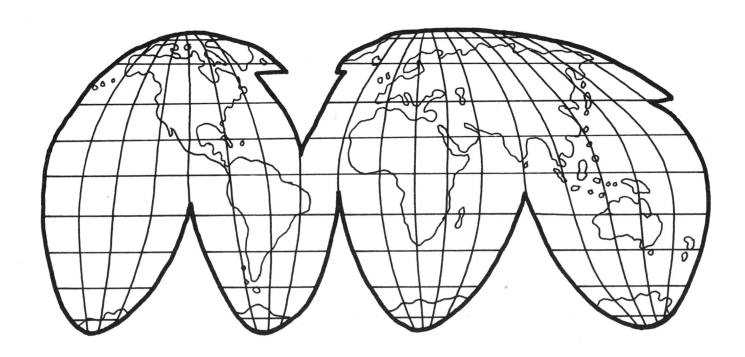

 # Where in the World?
A Mini Research Report

Select one country from which your paternal or maternal ancestors came to America, and complete the following personal data bank. This information will give you additional insight into your "origins" and help you become better "connected" to your "family tree."

1. The country I have chosen to "investigate" is _____.

2. The capital is _____.

3. Two interesting facts about the capital city are

    a. _____

    b. _____

4. Two specific geographic features (mountains, plains, rivers, etc.) of the country are

    a. _____

    b. _____

5. The type of government this country has is _____.

6. The current head of state is _____.

7. The currency is called _____,

    and the rate of exchange at this time is _____.

8. Two national (food) dishes are

    a. _____

    b. _____

9. Three important historical facts are

    a. _____

    b. _____

    c. _____

10. The main sport is _____ .

11. Two famous people from _____ are_____
                                (name the country)

   and _____ .

12. Two places I would like to visit in the country are

    a. _____ because _____

      _____ and

    b. _____ because _____

      _____ .

13. Three products _____ is famous for are _____ ,

   _____ and _____ .

14. Imagine that you have been hired by the tourist bureau of
   _____ to represent its "best image." On the next page,
     (your country)
   design a poster using cutouts from magazines, pictures from
   travel brochures, or your own illustrations to "sell" your ances-
   tral country to the rest of the world.

GA1421

53

GA1421

My State on the Map

Do a little research about the state in which you live, and complete the following chart. This list of facts will be an additional "piece of fabric" of your personal patchwork history, as well as be of interest to future generations.

1. I live in _____. It is abbreviated _____.

2. The capital is _____.

3. Its nickname is _____.

4. The governor is _____.

5. Two main tourist attractions in the state are

    a. _____

    b. _____

6. Two of its most famous citizens are _____

    and _____.

7. Two major league sports teams (name of club and sport) are

    a. _____

    b. _____

8. Two main products are

    a. _____

    b. _____

9. The flower is _____.

10. The bird is _____.

11. The tree is _____.

12. The animal is _____.

13. The most famous national park or historical monument in my

    state is _____.

14. Two additional interesting facts about the state are

    a. _____

    _____

    b. _____

    _____

15. Write a paragraph describing your state in its "most glowing"
    terms based on the mini research you have done to gather the
    above facts about your state.

    _____

    _____

    _____

    _____

GA1421

16. Make a collage to illustrate some aspect or aspects of your state of which you are especially proud. It could be a famous park, a well-known cultural center, a street known for its shopping, trade, or political importance, or any other reason.

56

My Time Line

Man's self-concept is enhanced when he takes responsibility for himself.

William C. Shutz

A time line or time chart is a means we use to record distinctive dates in human history or in the history of our own lives. Each person's "time line" is original. Use the time line below to pinpoint important events in your life. The time line starts with your birth and it ends with your present age. The middle part of the time line marks the halfway point of your life. On your time line, place those dates which are important to you. Next to each date, briefly explain its significance. For example, your time line might look like this:

1977   My birthday, January 28th
1983   Our family trip to Yellowstone National Park, June 15-June 20
1992   Broke my leg, trip to the community hospital emergency room, October 21

Date   **Event**

_____   My birthday _____

_____   _____

_____   _____

_____   _____

_____   _____

_____   _____

_____   _____

_____   _____

_____   _____

_____   _____

_____   _____

_____   _____

_____   Today _____

GA1421

Family Customs

Custom, then, is the great divide of human life.

David Hume

On the pages entitled "Who Am I?" and "I Am Unique," you examined the biological and psychological inheritance you received from your birth parents and considered how those contributions affected you, while enabling you to become "your own person." Now it is time to explore another aspect of who you are and see how it, too, affects you. This time you will be examining your cultural heritage and determine what role it plays in your life.

Culture is said to be the blending of language patterns, food customs, religious beliefs, political persuasions, and human adaptation to the surrounding environment. In other words, therefore, culture is the whole makeup of a particular society be it American, French, Japanese, or whatever.

You are the by-product of generations who were once reared in another culture and who brought that culture and its traditions with them when they came to America. In addition, to this, you represent someone who has been steeped in American culture and customs. So in you, both the "old" and the "new" have been forged in a strong, "I am my own person" mode.

After you have completed the following pages, you will have "sketched" for yourself, a more vivid, enriched picture of who you are, based on a knowledge of your special cultural heritage.

1. What language(s) is (are) spoken in your home?_____

2. Do your parents speak a language other than English? Y/N. If, yes, what language(s) do they speak? _____

3. Do your grandparents speak a language other than English? Y/N. If, yes, what language(s) do they speak? _____

GA1421

4. Do you know another languge? Y/N. *What is it?_____

   *If you don't know another language, but are taking or would like to take a foreign language, write it on the line for #4.

5. What are two favorite expressions used in your family? Who uses them? Write the expression on line a, and the person who says it on line b.

   a. _____
   b. _____

   a. _____
   b. _____

6. Tell about a distinctive family custom you have. It might take place at wedding, birthday, holiday or another special family day get-together. Maybe it is an annual family reunion. On the lines which follow, tell how the occasion is celebrated. Describe what is unique about it and who is usually the center of such celebrations (or of this particular occasion, wedding or birthday). First, draw a picture or put a photo of the "celebration" and then describe it on the lines which follow.

GA1421

Celebrating

60

7. Find a picture of a costume which is the traditional garb from your family's ethnic (country) background. Put it in the space below and give a brief description of it using the specific names given to different parts of the costume, such as a dirndl, kilt, or sari.

_____

_____

_____

8. Find a photo showing or illustrating the most memorable meal you have experienced with your family. (It might have been during a holiday such as Christmas or Hanukkah, it might have been a birthday party, it might have been a graduation party, or any other occasion.) Beneath the illustration, use the lines to describe the special foods that were served, the people who were there, and what made the day recorded as your most memorable meal.

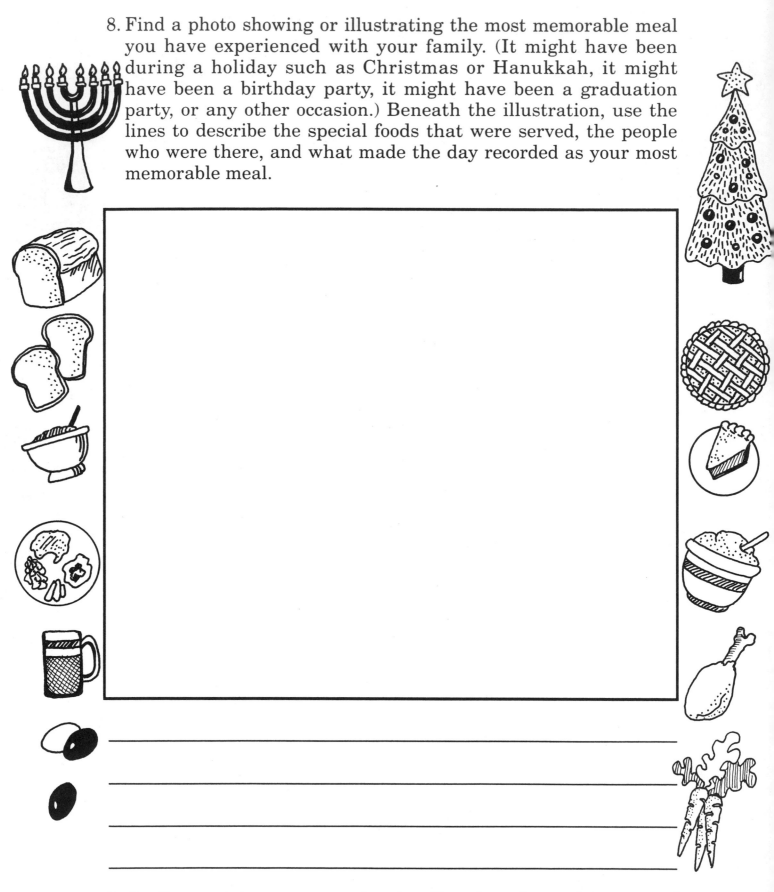

_____

_____

_____

_____

9. On the next two pages, write the directions for making two of your family's favorite recipes.

Favorite Family Recipe

1. Name of the recipe _____

Ingredients	Directions

GA1421

Favorite Family Recipe

2. Name of the recipe _____

Ingredients	Directions

Myths, Legends, and Folktales

All cultures are enriched with their own myths, legends, and folktales which have been passed down first from generation to generation usually through oral tradition. Now these stories have been captured in the written language of every nation. Find out one unique and appealing myth, legend, or folktale from your cultural background, and retell the story in your own words in the space provided on this page and the one that follows.

1. The story I have chosen is _____.
                                                (title)

2. It comes from _____.
                        (name the country or culture)

3. Here is the tale.

_____

_____

_____

_____

_____

_____

_____

_____

_____

_____

_____

GA1421

66

4. Illustrate the tale which you have rewritten.

5. Another part of our cultural heritage comes to us from literature. They are proverbs. A proverb is a short, wise saying used for a long time by many people, and which contains an element of truth. Two well-known proverbs are "Haste makes waste" and "All work and no play makes Jack a dull boy." Read some other proverbs, and then complete the following.

Two proverbs which I like a lot are (a) _____

_____ which means _____

_____

and (b) _____

which means _____

_____

6. Write and illustrate your own myth, legend or fable.

My _____ is called _____.
  (kind of tale)

GA1421

GA1421

 # Tell Me a Story...

Every family has stories to tell. Ask a grandparent, aunt, uncle, or older family friend to tell you a family story which needs to be remembered. The story may center on a special holiday, a family member, family secret, or whatever you wish. Record the story in the space provided.

_____

_____

_____

_____

_____

_____

_____

_____

_____

_____

_____

_____

_____

_____

_____

GA1421

_____

_____

_____

_____

_____

_____

_____

_____

_____

_____

_____

_____

_____

_____

_____

Told to me by _____ on _____ .

GA1421

Did You Ever?

Pioneer children did the things listed below. Put a check or highlight the boxes next to the activities you have done. Then ask your parents and grandparents to put checks or highlight the boxes next to the activities they have done. The comparisons should afford some interesting discussions "across generations."

	Me	Parent	Grand-parent
1. Carry firewood			
2. Gather eggs from a nest			
3. Make cider			
4. Grind coffee with a hand grinder			
5. Watch a horse being shod			
6. Paddle a canoe			
7. Feed chickens			
8. Dye yarn with plant dyes			
9. Split wood for a stove			
10. Ride in a covered wagon			
11. Churn butter with a wooden churn			
12. Pitch hay			
13. Spin wool			
14. Ride a horse bareback			
15. Take honey from a beehive			

GA1421

16. Go barefoot for the summer			
17. Milk a cow			
18. Make a willow whistle			
19. Sleep out doors overnight without a tent			
20. Saddle or harness a horse			
21. Go to bed by candlelight			
22. Make soap			
23. Go on a sleigh ride			
24. Bake bread			
25. Make maple syrup			
26. Pick wild greens			
27. Clean a fish			
28. Clean and pluck a chicken			
29. Shell corn with your hands			
30. Stuff sausage			
31. Have a doll with an apple head			
32. Have a quilting bee			
33. Cut off a chicken's head			

GA1421

34. Clean and light a kerosene lamp or lantern			
35. Make ice cream in a hand-crank freezer			
36. Clean your carpet with a carpet beater			
37. Live in a house with an out-house			
38. Eat hot oatmeal every winter morning			
39. Boil your clothes to get them clean			
40. Button shoes with a hook			
41. Light your Christmas tree with candles			
42. Fill a fountain pen from an ink well			
43. Take a bath in a wooden tub			
44. Play marbles			

List courtesy of the Barrington Historical Society, Barrington, IL 60010.

GA1421

Across Generations

...all that is not true change will dis-appear in the future society.

Anonymous

Interview your grandparents, an older friend, and parents and ask them to help you complete the following chart. It will help you measure the changes which have occurred across the generations. After you have seen the changes that have happened in a lifetime of your grandparents and parents, write down what is typical of your era so that future generations will know what your life and times were like. Each answer should be based on when the person responding to the topic was ten years old. For example, Franklin D. Roosevelt might have been President when one of your grandparents was ten years old, John F. Kennedy might have been President when one of your parents was ten years old, and George Bush might have been President when you were ten years old.

	Me	**Parents**	**Grandparents**
1. U.S. President			
2. Four important news events	a. b. c. d.		
3. Favorite song			

GA1421

	Me	Parents	Grandparents
4. List three household conveniences.	a. b. c.		
5. Favorite cartoon script			
6. Three major medical advances	a. b. c.		
7. Note three scientific discoveries.	a. b. c.		
8. Identify two popular forms of entertainment.	a. b.		

GA1421

	Me	Parents	Grandparents
9. Favorite subject in school			
10. Most popular car			
11. Three games played	a. b. c.		
12. What were fashions like? Major styles, colors or brands?			
13. Name three heroes of the time.	a. b. c.		
14. Name the three best sports' teams.	a. b. c.		

GA1421

	Me	Parents	Grandparents
15. Name three popular snacks. Include brand names.	a. b. c.		
16. Who were three favorite entertainers of the time?	a. b. c.		
17. List three popular magazines.	a. b. c.		
18. Name three famous movies.	a. b. c.		
19. Name two dances of the era.	a. b.		

GA1421

Cost of Each Item		Me	Parents	Grandparents
Loaf (lb.) of bread	1.			
1/2 gallon of milk	2.			
Pound of round steak	3.			
Dozen oranges	4.			
1 lb. bacon	5.			
Doz. eggs	6.			
5 lbs. flour	7.			
1 lb. pork chops	8.			
1 lb. butter	9.			
10 lbs. potatoes	10.			
1 lb. coffee	11.			
1 lb. margarine	12.			

GA1421

Cost of Living

Value is the life-giving power of anything; cost, the quantity of labor required to produce it; price, the quantity of labor which its possessor will take in exchange for it.

Munera Pluveris

Over the years the cost of living has skyrocketed. Economists tell us that by the year 2020 the price of a college education may reach upwards of $100,000 at a state-operated school. This kind of statistic is important for understanding what prices have been, what they are, and what they will be in the not-too-distant future. When you finish completing the following chart, you will no doubt wonder where the money-cost-spiral will end in the next generation.

Comparing the cost of essential goods and services from one generation to the next is a vital lesson in economics and a significant clue to what your forebearers paid for basic foodstuffs. On the following pages is a chart of basic items and their costs as noted in the U.S. Statistical Portrait of the American People for each decade from 1900 to 1990.

To use the chart, it will be necessary for you to find out when one or both of your parents and one or several of your grandparents were born. (If there is a major difference in birth years for your parents or grandparents, select one from each pair to portray on your chart, and make note of who you are using for your comparison.) Once you get the "birth years" of the two prior generation representatives, you will need to "round off" the years in order to complete the chart which follows. For example, if your maternal grandmother was born in 1934, "round off" the date to 1930. Then, if one of your parents was born in 1956, "round off" that birth-year to 1960, and use the data from that decade to complete the boxes on the chart under the "Parents" heading. Note that the data you are gathering is not "scientific," it is merely presented to show you how the "cost of living" has changed over three generations, and it will give you a feeling for how prices may continue to escalate in the decades to come. By doing more research into the economic conditions during the lifetime of your parents and grandparents, you will have a more fully developed picture of the soaring cost of living three generations have experienced.

Items		Me	Parents	Grandparents
Loaf (lb.) of bread	1.			
1/2 gallon of milk	2.			
1 lb. of round steak	3.			
Dozen oranges	4.			
1 lb. bacon	5.			
Doz. eggs	6.			
5 lbs. flour	7.			
1 lb. pork chops	8.			
1 lb. butter	9.			
10 lbs. potatoes	10.			
1 lb. coffee	11.			
1 lb. margarine	12.			

GA1421

Imagine that you have inherited five million dollars. Use illustrations to show how you would spend this "windfall."

GA1421

Comparative Cost of Living

Prices in cents per unit indicated.

Year	Bread (1 lb.)	Round Steak (1 lb.)	Bacon (1 lb.)	Eggs (dozen)	Milk Delivered (1/2 gallon)	Oranges (dozen)
1900	____	13.2	14.3	26.1	20.7	____
1910	____	17.4	19.2	33.7	16.8	____
1920	11.5	39.5	42.3	68.1	33.4	63.2
1930	8.6	42.6	42.5	44.5	28.2	57.1
1940	8.0	36.4	27.3	33.1	25.6	29.1
1950	14.3	93.6	63.7	60.4	41.2	49.3
1960	20.3	105.5	65.5	57.3	52.0	74.8
1970	24.3	130.2	94.9	61.4	65.9	86.4
1980	____	293.0	171.0	100.0	____	____
1990*	89.0	339.0	189.0	69.0	165.0	298.0

Year	Flour (5 lbs.)	Pork Chops (1 lb.)	Butter (1 lb.)	Potatoes (10 lbs.)	Coffee (1 lb.)	+ Marg. (1 lb.)
1900	12.5	11.9	14.3	14.0	____	____
1910	18.0	19.2	35.9	17.0	____	____

Year	Flour (5 lbs.)	Pork Chops (1 lb.)	Butter (1 lb.)	Pota-toes (10 lbs.)	Coffee (1 lb.)	+ Marg. (1 lb.)
1920	40.5	42.3	70.1	63.0	47.0	42.3
1930	23.0	36.2	46.4	36.0	39.5	25.0
1940	21.5	27.9	36.0	23.9	21.2	15.9
1950	49.1	75.4	72.9	46.1	79.4	30.8
1960	55.4	85.8	74.9	71.8	75.3	26.9
1970	58.9	116.2	86.6	89.7	91.1	29.8
1980	___	125.6	197.0	220.0	282.0	73.0
1990*	110.0	339.0	200.0	398.0	379.0	125.0

Key: *Prices supplied by Jewel Tea Company.
Information not available is indicated by a straight line.
To read the prices, move the decimal over two places. For example in 1900, a pound of bacon cost $.14 and in 1990 a pound of bacon costs $1.89.

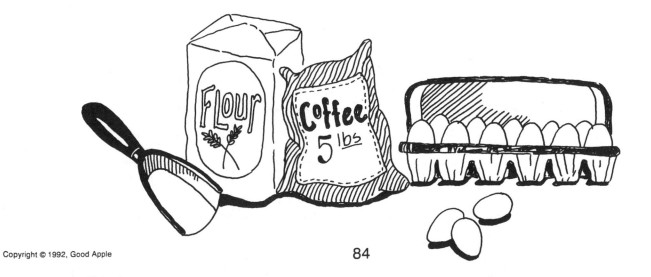

84

Family Heirlooms

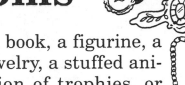

What is your most treasured possession? Is it a book, a figurine, a handmade quilt, a model airplane, a piece of jewelry, a stuffed animal, a box of letters from a friend, a collection of trophies, or something else?

Heirlooms are those treasures which have been handed down from generation to generation. They may include such things as a creamy-faced bisque doll; a brown leather family Bible; a yellowed-lace wedding dress; a gold, hand-tooled pocket watch; or anything your family holds dear and which has been in the family for some time. Every family has a few heirlooms. These treasures usually have more of a sentimental than monetary value. Sometimes they have both. Even if your family's heirlooms aren't worth a lot of money, they are worth a lot to your family. Learning about your family's "treasures," their history, their significance, and the place they hold in your family's legacy will give you another dimension of who you are.

1. What is your most treasured object? When did you get it? Who gave it to you? What is its history? What makes it valuable from your point of view?

_____

_____

_____

_____

_____

_____

_____

GA1421

2. Find your favorite family snapshot. Put the picture in the box provided or illustrate a favorite "snapshot." Beneath the picture, describe who is in it, where the photo was taken, what is happening, and why the picture is especially meaningful to you.

_____

_____

_____

_____

_____

_____

_____

3. Below put a snapshot or illustrate the oldest item your family has. Then describe it. Beneath the illustration, include such information about the item as how old it is, who it originally belonged to and especially why it is meaningful to your family.

87

4. Look around you and make a list of two items which are important to your way of life, and that you think will be important to the generation who will be living in the year 2121. Tell why you think each object will "withstand the test of time," or project your thoughts forward to the year 2121, and think of two inventions that will be in use then, which do not exist today. Give a brief description of these two items and illustrate each of them.

a. Item: _____

How utilized: _____

GA1421

b. Item: _____

How utilized: _____

5. What do you own that you treasure the most?_____
   (If you don't treasure anything at this time, but had the oppor-
   tunity to own something of "your dreams," list it as your "most
   treasured" for future family generations. Then tell why you
   want to leave this "treasure" for future family generations.

_____

_____

_____

_____

_____

GA1421

6. Here's (are) a picture(s) of my "treasure(s)."

Heraldry

The boast of heraldry, the pomp of pow'r,
And all that beauty, all that wealth e'er gave,
Awaits alike the inevitable hour:
The paths of glory lead but to the grave.

Thomas Grave

On October 14, 1066, an historic, fierce, and furious battle took place at the plains of Hastings, England. There King Harold of England met Duke William of Normandy (part of present day France). The conflict came about when Edward the Confessor, King of England, died and did not leave a direct heir to his throne. Thereupon, English noblemen selected Harold, the Earl of Wessex as king. This action brought an immediate and loud outburst from William, Duke of Normandy, who proclaimed that his cousin, King Edward, had promised him the throne at the time of his death. Tempers between the two powerful rivals flared, war clouds formed, and a threat of conflict appeared inevitable.

Harold's claim to Edward's kingdom was further aggravated by the king of Norway who also eyed the British kingdom. Upon hearing the Norwegian "sabers rattle," Harold led his men northward to assail the Norwegians head-on. With Harold preoccupied to the north, William realized the time was "ripe" for him to invade England and seize his "promised prize." Under Duke William's able command, the Normans set sail across the rough, rugged English Channel and safely landed on the shore next to the perilously steep British coast.

Learning that Duke William had come ashore and was marching on British soil, Harold turned his troops homeward to protect his southern flank. The ensuing battle was brutal, bloody, and costly. After weeks of war and countless casualties, the Normans outmaneuvered the English, and King Harold lay mortally wounded on the field, cut down by the razor-sharp arrow of a skilled Norman archer.

GA1421

The Battle of Hasting, as the conflict came to be called, not only gave British lands to the French, it also signaled a turning point in warfare. It gave rise to the medieval system of heraldry. During these times, men-at-arms began to paint their shields to symbolize their lord and to make sure that the side they were on was known to all on the battlefield. Prior to the creation of coats of arms, it was difficult to tell if a man charging at you with a pickax was your friend or your foe because the protective armor worn in combat hid each wearer's identity. The system of painting coats of arms came to be called heraldry.

Heraldry has a language all its own. *Blazon*, a French word, means "the description of a coat of arms." The first shields were simply decorated with two or three different colors. Over time coats of arms became quite elaborate in their designs and included "furs," "metals," lines, emblems, borders, objects, and mottoes.

Arms were later painted on buttons, etched on silver, embroidered on curtains, sewn on banners, carved into furniture, and made into seals which were used to validate all important documents, as they served as the document writer's signature. Today coats of arms appear on the flags of many nations, they rest atop the stationery of aristocratic families, they adorn the walls of people interested in genealogy, and they serve as "silks" or colored materials worn by jockeys and their racehorses at all track events.

Look over the Rules of Heraldry and then design your own coat of arms. If your family already has its own coat of arms, you may also want to include a copy of it in your autobiography.

Rules Governing Coats of Arms

1. Arms painted on shields had to be easily seen and recognizable from a distance.

Red   Yellow   Blue   Black

GA1421

2. Colors or tinctures used on shields had contrast. At first only five basic colors were used. They were
   a. red–gules
   b. blue–azure
   c. green–vert
   d. purple–purpure
   e. black–sable

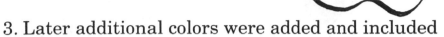

3. Later additional colors were added and included
   a. orange
   b. purple-red
   c. blood-red

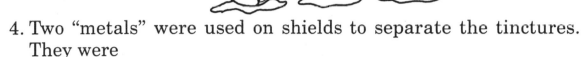

4. Two "metals" were used on shields to separate the tinctures. They were
   a. gold or "or," often represented by yellow
   b. silver or "argent," often represented by white

5. "Furs" called "ermine" enabled the shields to take on further individual designs. The furs added color and spots. The fur was not intended to be real but was to merely suggest the coat of an animal. The ermine represented the Arctic stoat whose summer coat is a reddish-brown and whose winter coat is white with a black-tipped tail.
   a. black spots on white–ermines
   b. white spots on black–ermine
   c. black spots on gold–erminois
   d. gold spots on black–pean

6. Vair patterns consisted of alternate white and blue pieces shaped in a variety of patterns. The vair was used by those who could not afford ermine. It was represented by the English squirrel which is blue-grey in color and sports a white under-belly. Vair patterns are therefore blue and white in color.

7. In the beginning a single line was used to divide shields in half either vertically or horizontally. By dividing a shield, owners were able to decorate them in two tinctures and two furs. Lines later took on greater variety and bars, crosses or chevrons came to be used on shields. These geometric configurations came to be called "honorable ordinaries." Some basic honorable ordinaries are shown below.

a. Saltire

b. Fess

c. Checky

8. Lines came to be narrower and provided shield designers with infinite possibilities for creating one-of-a-kind coats of arms. Two examples of lines and two examples of crosses follow.

a.    b.

9. Emblems on the surface of a shield were known as "charges." Position of the charges were carefully prescribed. Typical charges included

a. **Animals**
   horses
   elephants
   apes
   hedgehogs
   weasels
   rabbits
   lions
   bears
   hounds
   hippopotamuses

b. **Birds**
   falcons
   herons
   ravens
   eagles
   parrots
   ostriches
   swans
   ducks
   geese
   "martlet"

94

GA1421

c. **Monsters**

dragons	unicorn
griffins	centaur
cockatrices	sphinx
wyverns	opinicus

d. **Trees, grains, fruits, and flowers**

oaks, coffee, coconut, palm

wheat bundled in a sheaf

apples, pomegranates, grapes

roses, lily, thistle, a sprig of lime

e. Other charges consisted of
trefoil or shamrock

quatrefoil or four-leaf shamrock

cinquefoil or "five-leafed" shamrock

branches—laurel, palm, holly

10. Borders or bordures were also used to outline the shield's "field" or surface. Common borders were
Nebuly

Fleurs-de-lis

11. Human figures were also employed on shields. Examples of popular forms included
a. Images of kings

b. "Blind justice"

GA1421

12. Inanimate objects also made their way on heraldic fields. Among the more typical were the
    a. anchor
    b. arrow
    c. ecclesiastical hat
    d. battering ram
    e. hawk's lure
    f. torch
    g. harp
    h. tower
    i. battle-ax
    j. sun in splendor

13. Completing the shields were mottoes. They were originally written in Latin and later came to be enscribed in the language of the family's birthplace. Thus, mottoes appeared in French, Italian, and German. Mottoes were to be symbolic of the family's philosophy of life. Often references to God or virtue were utilized. Some mottoes grew out of war cries. The following are examples of mottoes used at one time or another by families of noblemen:
    a. Foremost if I can–Devant si je puis
    b. I will scatter my king's enemies–Sic dissipatio inimicos regis mei
    c. Yet hope is unbroken–At spes infracia
    d. Honor is my dowry–Mea dos virtus

In time, not only families, but organizations as well had shields with symbols to indicate what their organizations represented. For example, the carpenters' guild had a hammer, nails, and a saw on its shield. Wool merchant shields contained a ball of yarn, a pair of scissors, and a sheep in the center of it. Each guild or trade created its own shield. Today, coats of arms are commonplace and very popular. They are used by fraternities, scouts, church groups, hospitals, and other such clubs.

On the next few pages, you will be designing your own coat of arms. Even if your family has an official coat of arms, design one that you think represents who you really are. You can select your own colors, lines, objects, mottoes, and the like.

GA1421

My Coat of Arms

Using the information about coat of arms on the previous pages, complete the following data in preparation for creating your own coat of arms.

1. My tinctures are

   a. _____ chosen because _____

   _____

   b. _____ chosen because _____

   _____

   c. _____ chosen because _____

   _____

2. The style fur I have selected is _____.

   I chose it because _____

   _____

3. The honorable ordinaire I picked is called _____.

   It looks like this _____. I want this

   style of line on my coat of arms because _____

   _____

4. From the following list of charges select two or more which you want to incorporate into your coat of arms. Then in detail explain why you want each charge as part of your coat of arms.
   an animal, monster or bird
   a tree, grain, fruit or flower
   a border
   an inaminate object

GA1421

5. My charges are _____ and

_____ chosen because

_____

6. The motto on my shield is _____

because _____

7. Select three words which you feel typify your personality and which you will place on the "ribbon" beneath your shield. You might want to check back to the activity entitled "I Am Unique" if you need some ideas for words to describe yourself. Put your most important word-characteristic in the center of the "ribbon" under your coat of arms. Then write two other terms which you feel express your personality in the space to the right and to the left of the center-word. Be sure to tell why you selected each of these traits to represent you.

a. My main personality trait word is _____

because _____

_____

b. My second personality trait word is _____

because _____

_____

c. My third personality trait word is _____

because _____

_____

GA1421

My Coat of Arms

GA1421

My Medieval Manor

Let your mind wander back through the centuries to the Middle Ages. Imagine that one of your ancestors is the owner of a magnificent medieval castle and is planning a party for 300 friends. In the space provided, illustrate by words and/or pictures what the guests would have been served, what they would have worn, and how they would have been entertained. If you wish, give your ancestors and their castle names.

GA1421

My Hobbies and Collections

Almost everyone collects something. Among the items people collect are baseball cards, model trains, comic books, stamps, and postcards, to mention only a few. There are clubs and magazines for collectors who collect anything from advertising items to zinnia seeds. Collectors have an affinity for gathering together to display, barter, trade, swap stories, or seek advice from fellow collectors who share a common interest and language.

During the Great Depression of the 1930's, everything became scarce or outrageously expensive. Fearing the worst, people got in the habit of saving everything. They collected balls of string, pieces of aluminum foil, orange crates, glass jars; virtually anything that didn't spoil. Times were hard, and these people lived during difficult-to-imagine days and years. Hoarding was an acceptable way of life. Everyone set things aside for immediate or future use.

Today, Americans are inclined to be a throw-away society. In fact, two generations are currently living who never tasted the dastardly days of the 1930's; because of this, there is a tendency among Americans to dispose of out-of-fashion clothes, toys of childhood, even once-loved books. As we enter the 1990's and look toward the twenty-first century, Americans have begun to take a second look at their wastefulness. As evidence of this "new mood," each year there are more and more flea markets, garage sales, and auctions at which people are anxious to buy and "recycle" someone else's no-longer-valued or needed items. Sometimes the bargain hunters find long-sought-after treasures to add to their hobbies and collections.

Do you realize that turning a haphazard collection into an organized hobby is a pleasurable experience and that turning a collection into something meaningful gives collectors a lifelong pursuit of pleasure and wonderment? Recently a baseball card was auctioned for $45,000. Who would have thought that an item from a youngster's collection could become so valuable?

GA1421

1. List three things which you collect. If you do not have a hobby or collection at this time, what would you collect if you could?

   a. _____

   b. _____

   c. _____

2. How did you (or will you) get started with your collection(s)?

_____

_____

_____

_____

_____

_____

_____

_____

_____

_____

_____

_____

_____

GA1421

3. Make a list of hobbies or collections members of your family have or that friends of yours have.

Person   Collection/Hobby

a. _____   _____

b. _____   _____

c. _____   _____

4. Pretend that you can look into a crystal ball and see into the future. What do you think will become a collectible by the year 2010? Why?

_____

_____

_____

_____

_____

_____

5. Find out what kinds of collections at least one of your grandparents had? What has happened to the collection? Who has it?

_____

_____

_____

_____

GA1421

6. What do your parents collect? What got them involved in their collections? Who will inherit the collections?

_____

_____

_____

_____

7. Put an illustration of your favorite collection in the space provided, or put an illustration of a collection you would like to have in the space.

104

Memories

We must always have old memories, and young hope.

A. Houssaye

1. My happiest day was _____

_____

_____

_____

_____

_____

_____

2. I feel proudest about_____

_____

_____

_____

_____

_____

3. What I learned from a great disappointment is _____

_____

_____

_____

_____

_____

_____

_____

4. In the box below illustrate what makes you happy.

GA1421

School Days

The very spring and root of honesty and virtue lie in good education.

Plutarch

1. What is the name of the first school you attended?

   _____

2. How old were you at the time? _____

3. Tell about a teacher you have had who has changed your life in some way. How did the teacher change you?

   _____

   _____

   _____

   _____

   _____

   _____

   _____

   _____

   _____

   _____

GA1421

4. My favorite subject is _____ because

_____

_____

_____

_____

5. My fondest school memory is _____

_____

_____

_____

_____

_____

_____

6. The best thing I have ever done in school is _____

_____

_____

_____

_____

_____

_____

GA1421

7. Describe something funny or sad that has happened to you at school.

_____

_____

_____

_____

_____

8. In the box below illustrate one of your favorite school activities.

GA1421

9. You have been selected by the President of the United States to improve education in America. Describe what you think would make an ideal school. Tell about the classes, kinds and size; the teachers; the curriculum; the grading procedures to be used; and what your "philosophy" of education would be for this "school of the future." When you have completed this, you could send your ideas to the head of the Department of Education of the United States.

School of the Future

_____

_____

_____

_____

_____

_____

_____

_____

_____

_____

_____

_____

GA1421

10. Now that you have outlined how the "ideal" school will operate, design the ideal school plant below.

*My Favorite Things

1. Song	2. Movie
3. Store	4. Musical group
5. TV show	6. Actor/Actress
7. Kind of jeans	8. Fast-food restaurant
9. Food	10. Bar of soap
11. Hobby	12. Kind of chips
13. Sport	14. Place to vacation
15. Magazine	16. Cartoon
17. Car	18. Sports team
19. Soft drink	20. Snack
21. Vegetable	22. Artist
23. Author	24. Expression
25. President	26. Flower
27. Candy	28. Color
29. U.S. city	30. Chewing gum
31. Kind of pen	32. Radio station
33. Gym shoes	34. Ice cream flavor

*Be sure to write your favorite on the same line with the item to which you are responding. For example, next to #29, you might answer: 29. U.S. city–Chicago.

35. Below make a collage of some of your favorite things.

113

Friends and Friendship

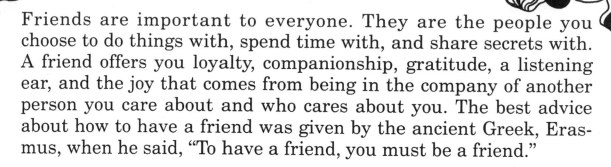

Friends share all things.
Pythagoras

Friends are important to everyone. They are the people you choose to do things with, spend time with, and share secrets with. A friend offers you loyalty, companionship, gratitude, a listening ear, and the joy that comes from being in the company of another person you care about and who cares about you. The best advice about how to have a friend was given by the ancient Greek, Erasmus, when he said, "To have a friend, you must be a friend."

1. Draw or put a picture of a friend in the box.

GA1421

2. A friend is _____

_____

_____

_____

_____

3. Tell about the first friend you can remember having.

_____

_____

_____

_____

_____

4. Who is your best friend now? _____

5. How long have you been friends? _____

6. Why is this friend important to you? _____

_____

_____

_____

_____

_____

7. Highlight with a marker or put a check next to those qualities which you think are important in a friend.

__ generous	__ honest	__ loyal
__ good listener	__ dependable	__ friendly
__ fun to be with	__ respectful	__ forgiving
__ sense of humor	__ trustworthy	__ helpful
__ sympathetic	__ athletic	__ good looking
__ willing to share	__ understanding	
__ can keep a secret	__ share same interests	
__ pleasant personality	__ have common values	

8. From the list of qualities you admire in a friend, explain how your friend has demonstrated two or three of these characteristics.

_____

_____

_____

_____

9. I like being with my friend when _____

_____

_____

_____

GA1421

10. In the box put some pictures or illustrate you and your best friend or friends enjoying special moments together.

11. Who knows you best? _____ Why?

_____

_____

_____

_____

_____

12. Staying with a friend _____

_____

_____

_____

_____

_____

13. Nobody knows, but one time my best friend, _____,

(name your friend)

and I _____

_____

_____

_____

_____

_____

GA1421

My Circle of Life

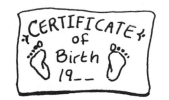

The years don't last as long as you think they are going to.

Walter Lippman

Select six special "moments" in your life. On the next page, illustrate each "piece of the pie" based on the following prompts.

1. In the first space, draw a picture of some event you want to recall that is important to you from the time of your birth to the age of five.

2. In the second space, illustrate something that happened to you between the ages of six and your present age.

3. Picture a major accomplishment in your life.

4. Show something good which has happened to you in the past year.

5. Draw your future occupation.

6. Illustrate your favorite activity or sport.

119

GA1421

My Circle of Life

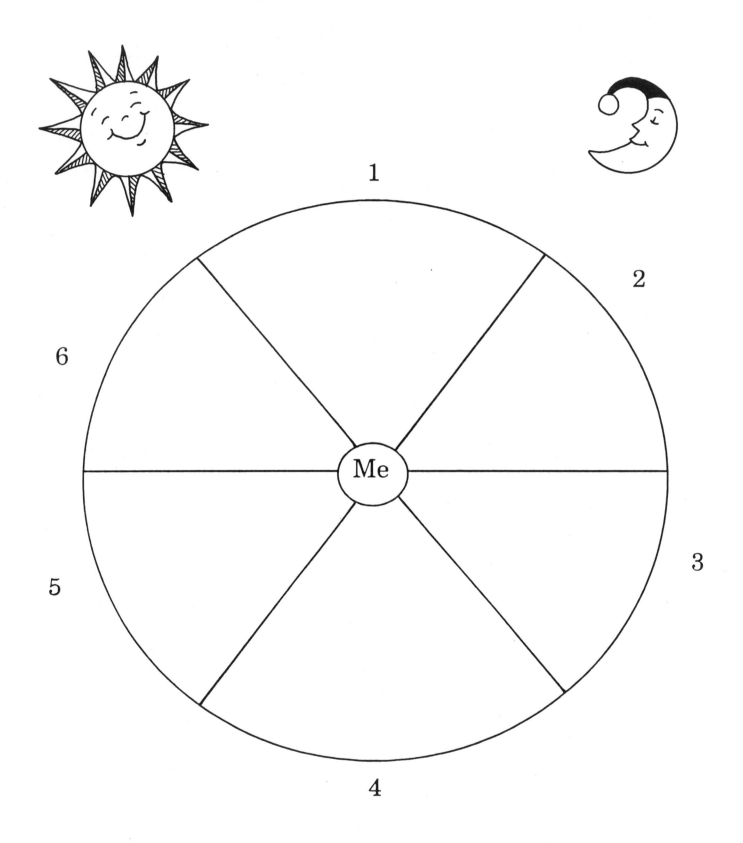

GA1421

Pets

Hardly anything is more fun than a pet. Part of the fun of any pet is knowing that it is yours, that it is there for you when you need a "friend," and that it accepts you unconditionally for who you are. In turn, a pet relies on you to feed it, give it attention, and to care for it, when it is well or when it is sick. In time, a pet can become your constant companion, your sidekick, your buddy.

Over the course of the life of your pet, it becomes another member of your family. A pet gives you years of shared camaraderie and wonderful memories. A warm relationship with a loved pet is a part of who you are.

*If you don't have a pet, select a pet you would like to have in order to respond to the following items. If you have more than one pet, it would be wise to select your favorite from among your pets so that your comments will focus on a particular pet.

My pet is _____.
(kind)

1. My pet's name is _____.

2. When did you get your pet? _____

3. Where did you get your pet? _____

4. How did you get your pet? _____

_____

_____

5. Who picked it out? Why was it chosen?

_____

_____

GA1421

6. What is the best experience you have ever had with your pet or a friend's pet?

_____

_____

_____

7. It has been said that pets make great friends. Give a specific example of when your pet was your "best friend."

_____

_____

_____

_____

_____

8. Animals make good movie stars. Think of a time when your pet did something so special that it could have had a lead role in a movie, or what is the best animal role you have seen in a movie? Why?

_____

_____

_____

_____

_____

_____

_____

GA1421

9. Put an illustration or a picture of your pet in the box, or make a collage of animals that you would like to have for pets.

 # My Pet(s)

My Heroes

Whoe'er excels in what we prize,
Appears a hero in our eyes.
J. Swift

The world is full of heroes. Some are famous like Abraham Lincoln, Susan B. Anthony or Martin Luther King, Jr. Others are not so famous. They are firemen, doctors, teachers, scientists, musicians—people from every walk of life who put their lives on the line to help others. We often learn of these heroes from accounts in the newspaper or on TV when their acts of bravery become the focus of daily news reports.

It is said that heroes are people who "seize the moment" and do what must be done in a given situation. Heroes are people who endanger their lives to save the lives of others. Someone might be trapped in a burning building, sitting on a thin ice-floe, or wedged between a too-narrow space, or in a car accident. Heroes come to the rescue of those in distress. But heroes represent people from all realms of our world. They may be politicians, athletes, giants of industry, or your next-door neighbor.

Literature is replete with stories of heroes and heroism. Some of them are humorous, like Toady in *Wind in the Willows*, who amuses us with his foolish antics when we read about his misadventure of trying to disguise himself as a washerwoman in order to escape from the police who are "hot on his trail." Other heroes are admirable in their ability to survive against incredible odds as we see in the character Karana in Scott O'Dell's, *Island of the Blue Dolphins*. Or we learn about heroes in comics where we meet Superman who can fly through the air, Batman who is able to employ wondrous gadgets to assist him in "saving the city," and Wonder Woman who can outsmart any threat to her safety merely by calling upon her wit, wisdom, and strength.

Heroes give us courage to be more than we can be, give us models we can emulate, make our world a better place in which to live. Who are your heroes?

GA1421

1. In your opinion, what is a hero? _____

_____

2. List three qualities, other than those mentioned in the narrative, which you think are necessary for someone to be a hero.

a. _____ b. _____ c. _____

3. Next to each characteristic which follows, highlight with a marker or put a check next to each trait which you feel a hero should exhibit.

_____ goodness   _____ courage

_____ strength   _____ humor

_____ diligence   _____ bravery

_____ popularity   _____ wealth

_____ outspokenness   _____ talent

_____ intelligence   _____ honesty

_____ thoughtfulness _____ helpful-
                                                ness

4. Who are your heroes? Name two of them and tell why you have selected each of them.

a. My first hero is _____ because

_____

_____

b. My second hero is _____ because

_____

_____

GA1421

5. The Chippewa Indians have a poem which describes heroism.
Read it and then respond to the comments which follow.

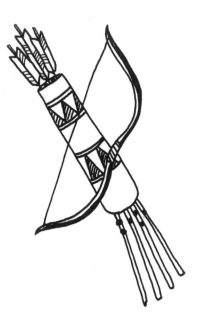

A Song of Greatness
When I hear the old men
Telling of heroes,
Telling of great deeds
Of ancient days,
When I hear them telling
Then I think within me
I too am one of these.

When I hear the people
Praising the great ones,
Then I know that I too
Shall be esteemed,
I too when my time comes
Shall do mightily.

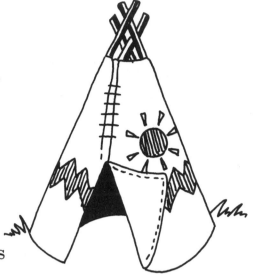

6. What "message" have the Chippewas given us in the poem "A
Song of Greatness"?

_____

_____

_____

7. Do the Chippewas believe everyone has the potential to be a
hero? Y/N. Do you think everyone can be a hero? Why or why
not?

_____

_____

_____

GA1421

8. Have you ever been a hero? Y/N. Perhaps you were one when you were baby-sitting or visiting an elderly grandparent. If you have been a hero, describe what happened and how you became a hero. If you haven't been a hero, do you think you would be able to act heroically if you needed to? Why or why not?

_____

_____

_____

_____

9. Another poem that focuses on heroism was written by the famous American poet, Ralph Waldo Emerson. He wrote a poem called "A Nation's Strength." In the poem, Emerson gives us a definition of *heroism*.

A Nation's Strength

Not gold, but only man can make
A people great and strong;
Men who, for truth and honor's sake,
Stand fast and suffer long.

Brave men who work while others sleep,
Who dare while others fly–
They build a nation's pillars deep
And lift them to the sky.

10. Who does Emerson consider to be heroes? Why are they heroes?

_____

_____

_____

GA1421

11. Do you think you could be a national hero? Why or why not?

_____

_____

_____

_____

12. Select someone in your family you consider to be a hero. (It should be someone other than the two heroes you have already written about at the beginning of this section on heroes.) Why do you think this person is heroic? Has the person ever performed a specifically heroic deed? Explain.

_____

_____

_____

_____

_____

13. If you could trade places with any hero in the world, who would it be?

_____ Why? _____

_____

_____

14. On the next page is a list of names of people who have been considered heroes at one time or another. Identify those people you recognize and highlight or put a check next to the names of the people you know something about.

President George Bush
Anne Frank
Albert Einstein
Leonardo da Vinci
"Magic" Johnson
M.K. Gandhi
Alexander Graham Bell
Christopher Columbus
George Washington Carver
Benjamin Franklin
General Grant
Walt Disney
Judy Blume
Michael Jordan
Thomas Jefferson
Florence Nightingale
Martina Navratilova
Lee Trevino
Michael J. Fox
Bill Cosby
Molly Ringwald
Bob Petty
Jacques Cousteau
Simon Bolivar
John Steinbeck
Andrew Wyeth
Charles Schulz
Cynthia Voigt
Elizabeth Blackwell
Joe E. Lewis
Lech Walesa
Mikhail Gorbachev
Maurice Sendak
Calvin and Hobbes
Luke Skywalker
Gwendolyn Brooks
Sir George Soliti
Mozart
Dr. Jonas Salk

Bishop Desmond Tutu
Mother Teresa
Susan B. Anthony
Jim Henson
Wayne Gretsky
Aesop
John Lennon
Beethoven
Copernicus
Oprah Winfrey
Madame Curie
Tom Cruise
Goya
Hippocrates
Tom Hanks
Nancy Lopez
Gen. Norman Schwarzkopf
Chopin
UB40
Ryan White
Bob Marley
Fred Savage
Nelson Mandela
Carl Sandburg
Frank Lloyd Wright
Claude Monet
Gary Larson
Scott O'Dell
Van Gogh
Danny Glover
Dr. Scuss
Jon Bon Jovi
Shel Silverstein
Chief Joseph
Bob Green
Chico Mendes
John F. Kennedy
Odysseus
Nolan Ryan

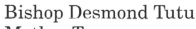
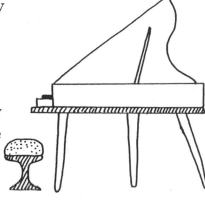

GA1421

15. From the list of heroes, select one person who you feel is truly a hero, do some research on your hero, and tell why you selected the person from the list. If you prefer to select someone not listed, do so. Just tell us about your "special" hero.

a. My hero is _____.

b. I would like you to know the following ten-plus facts about my hero's life:

_____

_____

_____

_____

_____

_____

_____

_____

_____

_____

_____

16. In the space below, make a collage of people you admire. You may use pictures out of magazines, or you may draw pictures of your heroes.

My Hero Hall of Fame

GA1421

Remembering Someone Special

Everyone has someone who is special to him. Think about someone who is special to you. It may be a parent, grandparent, teacher, or another adult friend. This person is someone who makes you feel special, who boosts your self-confidence, who takes the time to listen to you, who is interested in what you are doing, who gives you understanding, and who loves you for who you are. While the image of this special person is fresh in your mind, take the time to write a memory sketch of him or her.

1. My special person is _____
   (name the person)

   who is my _____.
   (tell what relationship the person has to you.)

2. Two words which best describe _____
   (name the person)

   are _____ and _____.

3. Recall a time when this special person came to your "rescue." What did you need? How did this person help you?

   _____

   _____

   _____

   _____

   _____

   _____

   _____

GA1421

4. When _____ came to my rescue, I felt
(write the name of the person from #1)

_____ because _____

_____

_____

5. The lesson(s) I have learned from _____ is (are)

_____

_____

_____

6. In the box, put a picture or make an illustration of your "someone special."

GA1421

An Acrostic

Poetry is simply the most beautiful, impressive, and widely effective mode of saying things.

M. Arnold

Use **your name** for the title of a poem. Write **your name** vertically down the page in the spaces provided. The first word of each line of the poem should begin with the letter you have written in each box. This kind of poem is called an acrostic.

When you write your poem, try to provide your readers with as much "texture" about you as you are able to supply. Your acrostic poem should describe you so that anyone reading it will have a clearly focused picture of you. Perhaps you would like to include in your poem something about your

physical features

personality traits

likes and dislikes

hopes and aspirations

secrets

favorite things

Here is a sample acrostic poem **about a cat named CAT**. If your name is longer than the boxes provided, use a nickname or an abbreviated form of your name.

Calico colored, a tabby I'm called.
Adopted from a shelter by a family who's loving and kind.
Treated to treats, when I do a trick, curled by the fire on a cold, windy night; a cat's life is "purr-fect" for me.

GA1421

My Acrostic

GA1421

Me Collage

I yam what I yam and that's all that I yam.
Popeye the Sailor Man

Collage is a French word which means "to paste." Cut out colorful pictures, words, and symbols which you think represent you and paste the items you have gathered in the box below. Be sure to allow the pictures to overlap and fill in the entire space. Words and symbols may be placed on top of the pictures, if you wish. The finished product should be an "image" of you. Perhaps you will want to include such things as

what you like to do   careers that interest you
people you admire   concerns you have
places you have been   things that make you happy
foods you like   things you think are beautiful

136

GA1421

I Have Changed

It has been said that the only sure thing in life is change. One of the purposes for writing your autobiography is to highlight the changes that have taken place in your lifetime. Changes that have taken place in the lifetime of your parents, grandparents, and even great-grandparents should also be acknowledged so each generation will leave a record of the changes that have taken place over time across generations. Awareness of these changes is an essential component in your life's story; it is a part of your history; it is a part of your autobiography.

1. What do you think has been the most important change in your life? Why is it the most important change?

_____

_____

_____

_____

_____

_____

2. On this page and continuing on the next, tell what you have done in your lifetime which has given you the greatest sense of satisfaction.

_____

_____

_____

_____

GA1421

_____

_____

_____

_____

_____

3. If there is one thing you could change about yourself, what would it be? Why would you like to change it?

_____

_____

_____

_____

4. What have you done that you are most embarrassed about? How old were you at the time? Were you alone or with others? If you were with others, what kind of an influence did they have on your decision to act the way you did?

_____

_____

_____

_____

138

GA1421

5. Identify two ways in which you have changed for the better.

_____

_____

_____

_____

_____

6. Illustrate some ways in which you have changed in the past five years.

GA1421

Someday I Want to Be

Selecting a career you want is quite important. It can determine if you will be happy, if you will earn a good living, and if you will ultimately make your life meritorious. It is not important that you pick your career today, or even tomorrow, but it is important that you begin to think about what you might like to do when your formal education ends. Certainly you can think of some jobs that interest you. Just keep one thought in mind, and that is, by the time you will be entering the "market place," there will be jobs available which don't even exist today. You could even "invent" a job that will be around when you are ready to work full-time.

At one time in the history of the world, it was assumed that children would follow in the footsteps of their parents; sometimes that is still the case today, but you have a great deal more freedom picking what you want to be than children of any previous generation. That is what makes thinking about your future so exciting. It lets you "run free with your imagination"; it lets you think of what "might be"; it lets you explore the possibilities of tomorrow's tomorrows.

1. My parents are _____.
   (list their jobs)

2. Would you like to have the same kind of job when you become an adult? Y/N. Why or why not? _____

   _____

3. When selecting an occupation that may last a lifetime, it helps to know what kind of person you are to help you make a decision about what you want to do with the rest of your life. For example, what kind of environment do you prefer to live in?

   Urban or rural? _____ Large city or small? _____

   What part of the country would you prefer to live in? _____

   Why? _____

4. Do you think you would prefer to be a boss with all the responsibilities that position demands, or do you think you would prefer to work for someone else? Explain.

_____

_____

_____

5. At this time, I think I want to be a (an) _____ when I become an adult.

6. If possible, try to interview someone who is currently working in the field that interests you. Make a list of facts that you find out about this person's job. You might like to find out the educational requirements for the job, the reason why the person you interview likes the job, its disadvantages, future growth in this field, how much you can expect to earn at the job, and other relevant data. List the facts you find out below. If you are unable to interview anyone, research the information in a library, or write to some agency for materials on the field that interests you.

The field that interests me is _____.

These are the facts I found out about it.

_____

_____

_____

_____

_____

GA1421

7. Use a collection of pictures to illustrate the kind of work environment which suits you, the kind of career choice or choices which interests you, and the kind of things you do well with your hands and/or mind. Then make a composite image entitled "Someday I Want to Be."

My Future

GA1421

Autographs

Obtain autographs from students in your classes or from anyone whose signature you value. If you wish, have them add a message for your "book of memories."

Autographs

Obtain autographs from students in your classes or from anyone whose signature you value. If you wish, have them add a message for your "book of memories."

144

Poem for Reflection

My roots are ancient and eternal,

My appreciation is for those who have gone before me.

My life is beautiful, bountiful, and blessed,

My hope is for peaceful todays and tomorrows,
  for this generation and for all who follow.

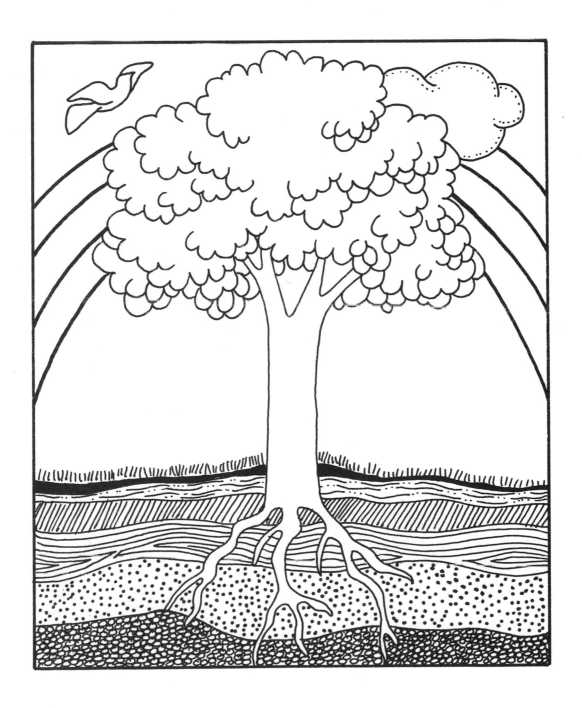

145

GA1421

My Keepsake Page

This keepsake autobiography was made while I was a _____ grade student at _____ School in _____. It

(city, state)

contains my thoughts, feelings, ideas, and creative energies. Looking back over my life, I have noticed how I have grown physically, psychologically, emotionally, and intellectually. I have learned about my role in my family, about my relationship to my living relatives, and about my position in my family tree. But most importantly, I have learned about the uniqueness of ME.

_____

Signature/Date

146

GA1421

Glossary

acrostic a poem which uses the first letter of a line in a horizontal fashion to create it

ad a shortened word for *advertisement*

album a book with blank pages or a book of collected items, such as a family album

ambidextrous able to use both hands with equal ease

ancestors one from whom an individual is descended

anonymous author is unknown

autobiography the story of a person's life written by himself or herself; a self-life writing

biological related to life or the life process; one's genetic inheritance

castle huge stone manor which included the noble's home, military surroundings, and surrounding grounds. Made during the Middle Ages.

chronological in the order in which things happen

chronology arrangement according to the order of time or happening; arranging and recording the dates of historical order of events in one's life; birth to death order

circa "about this time" or an approximate date. Used when the exact date is unknown.

collage a collection of different materials glued to a surface to make a picture or design

communication	the exchange of thoughts, information, or messages via telephone, letters, mail, radio, TV, or fax machines
comparative	measuring something in relation to something else, may be comparing what things cost in one generation to what the same things cost in the next generation
conveniences	anything that saves time and effort
culture	the customs, beliefs, arts, history, literature, and other areas of learning passed down from one generation to the next
currency	the form of money a country uses. The USA uses dollars, France uses francs, and Mexico uses pesos.
custom	something people do that is widely accepted or has become a tradition
deceased	no longer living; dead
environment	the physical and/or psychological surroundings in which one lives
ethnic	relating to people having a common language, culture, history and the like. For example, Polish, Spanish, Korean, or the like
family tree	genealogical chart showing one's ancestry or ancestry listing the names, date and/or place of birth and death
forebearers	one's ancestors, one's forefathers; grandparents, great-grandparents, great-great-grandparents, etc.
genealogist	one who traces the history of his or her ancestors

GA1421

genealogy	the study of one's ancestors, or forebearers
generation	a group of people born around the same time; a period of about thirty years, or the time between the birth of parents and the birth of their children
genetic	a part of one's biological or psychological makeup which has been passed on from one's biological parents and forebearers
given name	one's first name, such as Mary or John
governor	person elected head of each state in the United States
heirloom	a possession valued by members of a family and passed down from one generation to the next, such as a grandfather's clock, photo albums, a Bible
heraldry	the practice of devising, blazoning, and granting insignia and of tracing and recording genealogies. Commonly known as one's coat of arms.
hereditary	passing of characteristics from parents to off-spring
heritage	customs, achievements, and other things handed down from earlier generations; traditions
hero	a person admired for bravery or outstanding accomplishments
hieroglyphics	symbolic representation of words or ideas; ancient Egyptian writing
hobby	something a person does or studies for fun in his spare time. For example, some people make craft items for their hobbies.

illustrate	to add drawings, photos, or pictures cut out of magazines to explain or represent something
ingredients	something added or required to form a mixture, such as one of the main ingredients in chocolate chip cookies is chocolate chips
landmarks	prominent features of the landscape or of historical importance in one's life
mannerisms	one's speaking, acting, or behaviorial characteristics
maternal	of or like a mother; related through one's mother
medieval	a term used to describe the people, objects, events, and institutions of the Middle Ages which lasted in Europe from the 400's to the 1400's A.D.
memorable	worthy of remembrance, notable people or events in one's life
memories	storing or keeping things in the mind and bringing them back when needed or wanted
Middle Ages	period of history between ancient and modern times. See *medieval*.
muse	to think over, meditate, or reflect upon
myths, legends, and folktales	traditional stories dealing with gods or goddesses, or humans with super-human powers
nickname	a phrase or another name given in place of one's given or surname, such as Happy for Mike or Sue for Susan
origins	one's roots or beginnings; one's ancestors
paternal	of or like a father; related through one's father
portrait	a painting, photo, or visual representation of a person

GA1421

primitive	original, relatively simple people or culture
proverb	an old, often used saying that shows a known truth. "Many hands make light work" is an example.
psychological	related to the mind, to the mental process, characteristics inherited or acquired
relative	connected to another person by blood or marriage, such as an aunt, grandmother, or stepbrother
relevant	important; appropriate; pertinent
research	careful organized study of a topic, subject, or problem
residence	place where one lives
rural	living in, or having to do with the country
Sabbath	The day of the week that is used for rest and worship. Friday is the Sabbath for Moslems, Saturday is the Sabbath for Jews, and Sunday is the Sabbath for Christians.
sage	wise person or good advice
sibling	one's brothers or sisters
surname	one's last or family name, such as Smith or Jones
time line	important events in a person's life history which have been placed along a line which indicates a beginning, middle, and present time
traits	distinguishing characteristics; for example, bravery, honesty, cowardice or dishonesty
urban	of living or located in the city; having to do with a city or city life
verbal	of or having to do with words; ideas expressed in words, not in writing

GA1421

Bibliography

This book is intended to set the wheels in motion for you to record your family's history and add your history as an important component to that history. This bibliography lists the books used in preparation of this text, but your local library is full of additional sources to enable you to delve further into the fascinating hobby of genealogical research.

Arthur, William. *An Etymological Dictionary of Family and Christian Names*. New York: Gale Research Company, 1969.

Bailard, Virginia. *Ways to Improve Your Personality*. New York: W. Hill Book Company, 1965.

Bartlett, John. *Familiar Quotations*. Boston: Little Brown and Company, 1980.

Benjamin, Carol Lea. *Writing for Kids*. New York: Thomas Y. Crowell, 1985.

Brooke-Little, J.P. *An Heraldic Alphabet*. New York: Arco Publishing Company, Inc., 1975.

Brooke-Little, J.P. *Boutell's Heraldry*. New York: Frederick Warne & Co. Ltd., 1973.

Brown, Fern, and Andree Vilas Grabe. *When Grandpa Wore Knickers*. Chicago: Albert Whitman & Company, 1966.

Buehr, Walter. *Heraldry: The Story of Amorial Bearings*. New York: G.P. Putnam's Sons, 1964.

Chrystie, Francis N. *Pets*. Boston: Little, Brown and Company, 1964.

Dahl, Roald. *Boy: Tales of Childhood*. New York: Farrar, Straus, Giroux, 1984.

Evans, Bergen. *Dictionary of Quotations*. New York: Avenel Books, 1978.

GA1421

Fun and Games of Long Ago. New York: Americana Review, 1973.

Gilford, Henry. *Genealogy*. New York: Franklin Watts, 1978.

Greenberg, David. *Teaching Poetry to Children*. Portland: Continuing Education Publications, 1981.

Hacker, Andrew. *U.S. Statistical Portrait of the American People*. New York: Viking Press, 1983.

Hart, Carole (ed.). *Free to Be...You and Me*. New York: McGraw-Hill Book Company, 1974.

Harold, Robert, and Phyllida Legg. *Folk Costumes of the World*. Dorset, England: Blandford Press, 1978.

Hazen, Barbara Shook. *Last, First, Middle and Nick: All About Names*. Englewood Cliffs: Prentice Hall, 1979.

Historical Statistics of the U.S.: Colonial Times to 1970. Washington, D.C.: Bureau of Vital Statistics, 1975.

Katz, Marjorie. *Pegs to Hang Ideas On: A Book of Quotations*. New York: M. Evans and Company, 1973.

Lambert, Eloise, and Mario Pei. *Our Names: Where They Came from and What They Mean*. New York: Lothrop, Lee & Shepard Co., 1985.

Legrand, Jacques. *Chronicle of the 20th Century*. New York: Chronicle Pub. Inc., 1987.

Lee, Mary Price, and Richard S. Lee. *Last Names First...and Some First Names Too*. Philadelphia: The Westminster Press, 1985.

Levinson, Leonard Louis. *Bartlett's Unfamiliar Quotations*. New York: Cowles Book Company, Inc., 1971.

Macaulay, David. *Castle*. Boston: Houghton Mifflin Co., 1977.

Manning, Rosemary. *Heraldry*. London: A. & C. Black Ltd., 1975.

McGough, Elizabeth. *Who Are You?: A Teen-ager's Guide to Self-Understanding*. New York: William Morrow and Company, 1976.

GA1421

Meltzer, Milton. *A Book About Names*. New York: Thomas Y. Crowell, 1984.

Miller, M.A., Dorothy. *The Middle Ages*. New York: G.P. Putman's Sons, 1935.

Moody, Sophy. *What Is Your Name?* London: Gale Research Company, Book Tower, 1976.

National Genealogical Society. Washington, D.C.

Newbecker, Ottfried. *A Guide to Heraldry*. New York: McGraw-Hill Book Co., 1979.

Nevins, Albert J. *A Saint for Your Name: Saints for Boys*. Huntington, Indiana: Our Sunday Visitor, Inc., 1980.

Nevins, Albert J. *A Saint for Your Name: Saints for Girls*. Huntington, Indiana: Our Sunday Visitor, Inc., 1980.

Nisenson, Samuel. *The Dictionary of 10,001 Famous People*. New York: The Lion Press, 1966.

Norton, Donna E. *Through Children's Eyes*. Columbus, Ohio: Charles E. Merrill Pub., Co., 1983.

Peter, Lawrence J. *Peter's Quotations: Ideas for Our Time*. New York: William Morrow and Company, 1977.

Pine, L.G. *The Story of Surnames*. Rutland, Vermont: Charles E. Tuttle Co., Inc., 1966.

Rico, Gabriele Lusser. *Writing the Natural Way*. Boston: Houghton Mifflin Company, 1983.

Roberts, Kate Louise. *Hoyt's New Cyclopedia of Practical Quotations*. New York: Funk & Wagnalls Company, Inc., 1922.

Salny, Roslyn W. *Hobby Collections A-Z*. New York: Thomas Y. Crowell Company, 1965.

Shankle, Ph.D., George Earlie. *American Nicknames: Their Origin and Significance*. Second Edition. New York: The H.W. Wilson Company, 1955.

GA1421

Smaridge, Nora, and Hilda Hunter. *The Teen-ager's Guide to Collecting Practically Anything*. New York: Dodd, Mead & Company, 1960.

Smith, Elsdon C. *American Surnames*. New York: Chilton Book Company, 1969.

Smith, Elsdon C. *New Dictionary of American Family Names*. New York: Harper & Row Publishers, 1973.

Stewart, George R. *American Given Names*. New York: Oxford University Press, 1979.

Summerlin, Randy (ed.). *Big Book of Baby Names and Announcements*. Tuscon: HP Books, Inc., 1983.

Thomas, Frank P. *How to Write the Story of Your Life*. Cincinnati: Writer's Digest Books, 1986.

Tchudi, Susan and Stephen. *The Young Writer's Handbook*. New York: Charles Scribner's Sons, 1984.

Unstead, R.J. *Living in a Medieval City*. Reading, Massachusetts: The Globe Co., 1971.

Webster's New Geographical Dictionary. Springfield, Massachusetts: Merriam-Webster, Inc., Pub., 1984.

Wells, Jane, and Cheryl Adkins. *The Name for Your Baby*. Richmond, Virginia: Westoner Pub., 1972.

Westin, Jeane Eddy. *Finding Your Roots: How Every American Can Trace His Ancestors, at Home and Abroad*. Los Angeles: 1977.

Welty, Eudora. *One Writer's Beginnings*. New York: Warner Books, 1983.

GA1421

A good source for obtaining needed genealogical information can be obtained by writing to the Bureau of Vital Statistics of each state. In addition, most useful sources in your efforts to locate information about your ancestors will be found in specialty libraries and from genealogical societies. Especially useful are branches. They have the most complete genealogical records of any organization in the world. You may write to their headquarters for the location of the branch nearest you at this address:

Church of Jesus Christ of Latter-Day Saints
50 East North Temple Street
Salt Lake City, UT 84105

National Genealogical Society
1921 Sunderland Pl. N.W.
Washington, D.C. 20036

Another point to keep in mind when contacting any public agency in search of data about your ancestors is to be sure to include as much of the following information as you are able:

1. The full name of the person for whom you are searching

2. The sex and race of the person

3. The names of his or her parents. Remember to include the mother's maiden name.

4. The month, day, and year of the person's birth, death, and/or marriage

5. The town, county, state, and hospital (if known) in which the person was born